SKIPPING STONES

Adrienne Stevenson

Marie-Andrée Auclair

SKIPPING STONES

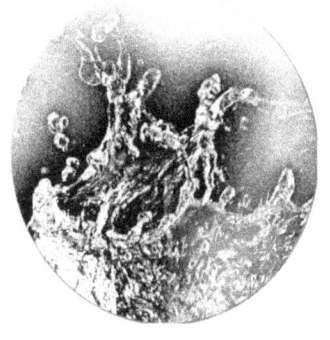

The BumblePuppy Press

OTTAWA, CANADA
2024

The BumblePuppy Press

Skipping Stones. This book is a collection of poetry. Any references to historical events, real people, or real places are used fictitiously. Other names, characters and events are products of the authors' imaginations, and any resemblance to actual events or people, living or dead, are strictly coincidental.

Text copyright © 2024 by Adrienne Stevenson and Marie-Andrée Auclair.

Cover by The BumblePuppy Press. Cover image by TrevorImages, courtesy of CanStockPhoto.com.

All rights reserved, including the right to reproduce this book or portions thereof in any form whatsoever. The scanning, uploading, and electronic sharing of any part of this book without the permission of the publisher is unlawful piracy and theft of the author's intellectual property. Please don't do it. If you would like to use material from the book (other than for review purposes), prior written permission must be obtained by contacting the publisher at inquiries@bppress.ca.

Skipping Stones is published by:

The BumblePuppy Press
Station E, P.O. Box 4814
Ottawa ON K1S 5H9
Canada

National Library of Canada cataloging in Publication Data:

Skipping Stones: ISBN: 978-1-7387598-5-9

An ebook edition of this book is also available: 978-1-7387598-7-3

First edition

Contents

9	Skipping Stones
10	Trust Fund
11	Flux
12	A Matter of Intensity
13	Outlook
15	Discovery
17	A Conversation Between Image-Makers
18	Comfort Zone
19	How to Phrase a Smile
21	Sign Language
22	Stereotype
23	Cartographer
25	A Garrisoned Vale
26	Games We Play
27	Orbits
29	Down the Pub
30	What We See
31	Heart of Oak
32	Once Verdant
33	Threadbare
34	Fugue State
36	Collage
38	Composition
39	Loom
40	Unearthing Myself
42	Positive Spin
43	The Right Stuff

44	Where I Am
45	And Again
47	Scars
48	Soot
49	Kaleidoscope

Publication Credits
About the Authors
Acknowledgments

Skipping Stones

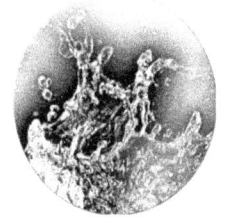

Skipping Stones *Auclair & Stevenson*

You lie on a sandy beach: the sand is sun-warm
pricks your skin with finely ground glass specks
that the lake has not yet licked smooth
while worn-flat pebbles remember the granite mountain
that looms over your lonely shore.

Our smooth stones, each fitting the heart of our palms
trace low arcs above the water
touch and rebound until their energy is spent.
Then one of us sacrifices the next stone
to the god of placid waters.

You sit, arms akimbo, fingers idle, attentive
to clouds and birds, the patterns of flight
and wind, the peaceful motion of branches and leaves
that draws you to its breath, to yours
and you feel yourself taking root like grass and trees.

That is what we do, throw our poems on the page
of a common lake, what sinks quickly is culled
what uncoils its energy in many rebounds stays,
a blended poem for our venture, another bird in the sky.

Trust Fund *Stevenson*

a change of world is coming
we cannot stop it or even interfere
without precipitating its arrival
—it has been on its way a long time

symptoms of the upheaval
pile up daily—society's fringes
restless, rumbling, ranting
chanting conspiracy theories

will we avoid the lawlessness
that so often accompanies change?
our eroded infrastructure
might not cope with turmoil

I take heart in my fellows
whose forebears endured war
disease, oppression, hate
survived, remained strong

we are the world's trust fund
we are the reservoir of courage
we will resist anarchy, those who would
tear us down, and we will rise

Flux   *Auclair*

Pulsing wordless
emotions, my heart
rushes crimson vigour
through a maze
of vessels, arteries
grand boulevards,
narrow streets
and dead-ends
circuits a Monaco track
roars
until the wave
of the checkered flag.

Out of an infinite vastness
random possibilities
mesh into a web
I call fate.
I push it away in fear
as if it were not me,
not my heart beat
that resonates
on the cosmic drum.

Yet, my heart, small as a fist
beats a tattoo against its cage
and holds me in the flow
of kokoro.

A Matter of Intensity   *Stevenson*

soft light grows over the city
its sharp edges blurred as dawn begins
noon's stronger rays reveal
harsh lines, only for them to fade again
as dusk filters back to shadow

peace and tranquility are easily disturbed
gentle glow of kindly fires
can be over-fuelled, become conflagration
as disruptive elements set fire to civilization
once burning, difficult to quench

somewhere between shadow and brilliance
ambience and glare
beam and glower
civilization and anarchy
there is just enough light to read by

Outlook *Auclair*

A cardinal ruffles the air
I trace its red flash through swinging branches
flutters of green, the echo of its song.

My eyes scan the small space
around my boots, each step
the centre of a brief circle.
This is what I care about
this morning.

The path, vague pattern
of rocks, leaves and twigs
that sneak between soaring trunks,
does not exist until I walk it.

I follow the crooked line
that my eyes cast ahead.
I climb steps made for drunken giants
who thirst for my devotion
which I give, which I gladly give
afraid of the loose stone
the pretty mossy one
and the tug of my backpack.
Balance, no longer a given,
demands scrutiny.

When at last I sit, unhook my pack
take slow breaths, my body warm
and thrumming, I notice

an absence of inner verbiage
no volley of thoughts
to keep me company. Instead
my mind broadens over
rhythmic waves of hills
calm and vast
and dissolves.

Discovery *Stevenson*

children's eyes open wider
see more possibilities
colours brightest
shapes malleable
flavours pungent
textures novel
music expansive
every sensation honed
to its finest peak

children create their own rituals
find meaning in small things
until adults, institutions
constrain, crush them
insist they conform to some norm
unperceivable by open eyes
paths leading only to darkness
constricted ways of thinking
opportunities forever lost

what could the world become
if we loosened those bounds
guided with kindness
steered gently, by example
fostered knowledge, understanding

instead of indoctrination, ignorance
lies-to-children?
a better place, I think
a discovery worth making

A Conversation Between Image-Makers *Auclair*

What you write is only self-reflection
my painter-sister says with a slanted smile
all art is self-portrait.

She dents my shield with an uncanny knack:
—am I another unveiled painting hanging on the wall
isn't she there too—

Don't we choose our interpretation? I say.

I inhale atoms from her breath
exhale some of my own
mine, hers, inaccurate possessives.

We transmit anonymous molecules
from fighters sparring
from saints some love, to each other.
The air grazes our vulnerability.

She lifts her chin, dams the wet shimmer
behind her lower eyelids.
Children, she says, disappear an iota at a time
that's why

I painted my girl walking away.

Comfort Zone   *Stevenson*

She abhors crowds
prefers a cozy circle
a few intimate friends
sometimes one is too many.

He is gregarious
never so happy as at the centre
chatting up new people
he never misses a chance.

Quite by happenstance
they meet in a café
over his cappuccino (extra foam)
and her triple shot.

Do opposites attract?
They spark each other
into uncharacteristic chatter
on her part, silence on his.

They agree to compromise:
she still lives alone; he visits often
scratching an itch
neither knew they had.

How to Phrase a Smile   *Auclair*

We chat face to face
word-build our friendship

my hands—her blindness
renders them mute—
still punctuate
my words
my forty-three facial muscles
provide no
short-cuts.

So I funnel
gestures
and grins
into speech
rely on my vocal cords
to relay
more feelings.

I face a choice
spell out betray
—her, myself, both of us?—
shun body short-hand for a verbal detour
or
skip over
translating silent tears
disgusted frowns, happy nods.

The strange thing is
while I watch her

have no visuals
of me
I watch myself
more
closely.

Sign Language   *Auclair*

My body speaks its new language
of delayed aches and unfamiliar
stiffness. No more
elbows grazing my toes
just head between my knees
legs folded at a straight angle.

My old words hold the new truth
of my body. *I cannot*
used to mean *I could* but
I don't feel like it, don't want to
don't have time, maybe I am lazy
and *I cannot.*

Now *I cannot* is humbling admission
of a physical constraint
impossible to defeat.
My faithful servant speaks
in signs of wear that I cannot ignore:
it calls for more kindness.

Stereotype

Stevenson

I try to please these desperate girls
that call on me from their dark corners

I give them silk dresses, turn mice
to footmen, pumpkins to coaches
but what do I get in return?
no thanks or caresses for a tired old woman
who has spent her magic on the ungrateful wretches
no, they run off with the first prince
to pick up their dropped handkerchief or lost slipper

I will waste no more time on these girls
but return in my next incarnation
as a wicked witch
and enjoy myself for a change

Cartographer *Auclair*

I watch you
pencil me
with supple strokes

If, or better, when
you want to know someone
—you, me—
draw a map
indefinite frontiers
to embrace shifts
in promises

sketch too
meandering veins
of navigable waters
topographical arteries
to contour obstacles
mountains, as necessary
over-edge to adventures

with graphite, coloured pens
define known bodies
landscapes of familiar roadways
and barely felt trails
through green forests
plot paths across untamed land
—allow for fence mending—

assign hues
—a colour scale or two—

rainbow insets for legends
before spreading an overlay
to protect delicate boundaries
consider aquarelle
after draw-dragging some truths

between your designs and mine
then, satisfied, add India ink.

A Garrisoned Vale   *Stevenson*

the valley is as deep as a damaged heart
guarded round with nettles and broken glass
thorn bushes and false smiles
entry barred to all but a chosen few

the guardian who lives there
must not be confused with the chosen
although he has given them access
he guards his own silences

who shall unwrap long-hidden secrets
and expose the guilty in their shame?
the guardian is wary of giving up the key
he remains steadfast, in shadow

come, you who suffer and despair
join the ranks of the secret-keepers
hoard your precious pain
be sheltered in this vale

then, when self-love resumes
take your pain and speak it
to those who need to hear
you will be believed

Games We Play   *Stevenson*

the match between us was not scripted
no duration was established
no point system assigned, no rules set

nobody was picked for a team
although teamwork is required
we struggle to maintain our own space

frequently clashing over minutiae
from time to time we meld
into near-unity, so briefly

we remember ancient grievances
fail to celebrate joy for long
but welcome its recurrence

our gazes sometimes wander
yet revert like migrant birds
shuttlecocks on a return of service

we are collaborators and opponents
the ball passes back and forth between us
what is the state of play?

Orbits   *Auclair*

We pedal our three-wheelers on parallel paths
concentric circles around each other
on home lawns. Parents applaud
then call us home.

We grow strong calves, balance and speed
and the sweet-talk
of wind in our ears
silences parents' warnings.

Our paths meander
as do our conversations
that roamed an imagined atlas
along tamed bicycle lanes.

We glory on racing bikes
invent beacons
to mark a joint memory map
connive courses through the unknown

to reveal goals we call ours.
We push away from the banal
to plot trajectories to bliss
certain we'll conquer the world.

We grow up, claim our acre of land
grow roots, acquire four-wheel vehicles.
The children get a dog, and we,
memberships, tenures and mortgages.

We spin on stationary bikes
until we slow old, mosey on
into retirement on a tandem bike
that we will trade for second-hand tricycles.

Once again, we ride in circles.
Grandchildren slalom on the paved alleys
of our old folk residence. They cheer us on
until the sun sets and it is time to go home.

Down the Pub   *Stevenson*

going down the pub used to mean
a fug of lovely smoke, before
it became bad for us, several pints
and we wouldn't care, even now

down the pub we could let go
sing at maximum volume
each in our own key, syncopated
to idiosyncratic rhythms

tables filled with trays of draft
seven-ounce glasses or full pints
depending on the establishment
foam flowing over brims

the best barkeeps pulled pints full
no skimping on the golden brew
live music on selected nights
dancing hindered by sticky floors

down the pub were the best of times
futures still unobstructed
no bars yet erected in our minds
fun our only objective

What We See   *Auclair*

I see wrinkles on their faces
when they say *you're not any younger.*
I don't see wrinkles on my face:
I am still thirty inside, don't they see?

I see they worry
at my loss of youth.
If my youth disappeared
how secure is theirs?

I see they avert their eyes
push me into an invisible quarantine.
I am no longer part of "us"
and they are "they" to me.

Don't we see we are the same?
I see we fail to be curious
about the scary territory of aging
that edges our future.

I see wrinkles on their faces
and wrinkles on mine.
We carry on bravely when we can
the weight of our efforts unseen.

Heart of Oak   *Stevenson*

outside my office window, columnar oak
sends stray branches east and west
as if seeking others to hold hands
sometimes reaches out to me where I sit
in entreaty for its leaves to become words

the branch outside my cottage bedroom
also reached out to me, beckoning
for a friend to come and swing
on the two ropes and plank
hung from its horizontal strength

from the shoreline, a sapling my height
a descendant of that protective oak
was taken by my father to our house
found welcoming soil and flourished
became haven for squirrels and birds

my life can be measured in oak tree friends
our overlapping lifespans share seasons
the oaks of my life twine their branches round me
reckon the truth of my grade-school's motto
great oaks from tiny acorns grow

Once Verdant *Auclair*

In twin bathroom mirrors, haloed
by artificial light, you and I glimpse
the unfamiliar faces we've acquired,
only your gaze on me familiar.

Winter scours trees to charcoal skeletons.
A tarnished sky filters the sun
down to a feeble yellow orb.
We've slowed our pace, withered
like mounds of leaves, rain or sleet battered.

Our twilight plunges toward night.
We huddle into sweaters near the hearth,
burn our summer memories
along birch logs that spit stars.

Our eyes peer through glasses
that fail to erase the sepia tone
our yellowing corneas foist
on our scenery. Shadows
spill the secrets of bone.

In mirrors, our fingertips check
what our eyes fear, the nakedness
of your skull, mine, our discoloured skin.
We wish for kinder lights,
and seeing less is our last-minute blessing.

Threadbare   *Stevenson*

We were talking about the old days
I didn't quite catch the gist ...
What was that you said?

I've been around for thirty-three
thousand days; known you more than half that
We were talking about the old days

There's no need to shout
I can still hear you
What was that you said?

I came in here for a reason
Must have been to see you
We were talking about the old days

Remember the time when we ...
Now where did I put my keys?
What was that you said?

Hello, hello old friend
How lovely to see you again
We were talking about the old days
What was that you said?

Fugue State *Stevenson*

convention has it that fifty years ago
is considered history—disconcerting to me
since I grew up in historical times
unaware then that this would be so

fewer than three billion humans lived
when I was born—as of today
near eight billion, threefold increase
as human population overwhelms

the planetary petri dish
our footprints multiply by exponents
no more pitter-patter—gargantuan stomp
measures our collective tread

as more of my life becomes history
the future seems more illusory
pace of alteration of the current world
too rapid to forecast our destiny

these thoughts consume me at times
when my reality thins, the illusions
of comfort, sanity come under fire
I doubt my belonging in my own skin

I walk down the hall, wondering where I am
whose life I have stepped into, vaguely aware
of the history that surrounds me
but I don't recognize the assemblage

the compendium of things in these rooms
is unfamiliar, was it really me who amassed
all these books, artworks, recordings?
surely they belong to someone else's history

Collage   *Stevenson*

She wants to be able to see him
bending over his work, as colours move
from the palette to the canvas
or watch the photo taking form
under layers of liquid; he eases it out
with gloved hands and sets it to dry:
it will form a part of the collage.

There is always a dab of blue
somewhere, even in what looks
like total redness; it is the sky
or his eyes, or a mountain lake,
or maybe just the notion of blueness
that transcends into peace.

His work is not peaceful
nor is his life, but
he is always eager to explore
and only keeps that hint of blue
to remind him that all things
come to rest in the end.

She wants to reassure him
that he is loved—he never seems
to believe this wild notion;

her heart sends a message of hope,
but it is lost
in the mass of transient hearts

crowding around him like
elusive blue butterflies
at the golden honeypot.

Composition   *Auclair*

Familiarity shrinks its object: Hexies
I call the hexagons I cut from worn cloth,
like I call you Sweetie, Honey Bun,
any endearing diminutive. I patch-stitch tapestries
and bedspreads and clutch-purses
full of memories out of hexagons taken
from your shirts, my skirts, our curtains,
the bright and the dark
and the avid needle pricks my thumb, wets
the thread with my blood.

Loom   *Auclair*

I weave on an invisible loom, framed
by wooden directives and genetic strands.

As the bee flits about in search of gold
and silver honeyed threads, and settles
for tin and lead, I bumble around
twining strands, one at a time
in and out of given patterns
warp over, weft under, weaving
the tapestry of my lifespan.
Snags, unavoidable, add texture
and become signature or scar.

How easily I forget, when I aim
for mastery, that I live like Damocles
under the fated hair that keeps a sword
from ripping my fabric.

Unearthing Myself   *Stevenson*

I rummage in dustbins
in search of myself, my past
supposed to inform my present
and predict my future, random
accretions of words, images
blink data points, poke
the edges of my brainbox
trigger unwished-for memories

topmost layers near unpierceable
require jack-hammers, sharp picks
at first dents, then pits appear
pock-marks on toughened surface
only persistence penetrates
reveals concealed entrance points
one-way exits to pry open

memory elusive, fleeting, escapes
before fully realized, shy to be seen
reluctantly revealed, some bright
some dreary, laced with pain
some drowned in mundane oceans
of too many repeated days

I, as analyst, never complete
the process of self-excavation
but dredge up faulty recollections
sift through elusive traces
feel the truth slither away
from my prying mind

Positive Spin *Auclair*

Who would not
tell tales of convivial comfort
deny daily decline?
You'll get better, they promise.

Who would not
spin stories of flexible solace
out of truths that our memory
massages with each iteration,
and water flowers at the head of graves?

We erect word ramparts against chaos
cement mortar and rubble into consensus
slap bright coats of paint on bollards
any way we can to dress up
the unsightly certainty
that we too are scared?

The Right Stuff   *Stevenson*

events are already over
when you take the first
step towards them
planning, anticipation
excitement before things happen

moments of happening
too fleeting
to register satisfying details

hear the music in all voices
see what you want to see
not what is there

invent the world
so you can know it
as the stuff of which
dreams are made

Where I Am   *Stevenson*

school children write their names and addresses
in textbook flyleaves, specifying location
in a list that spirals out from street, town, province
country, continent, planet, star system, galaxy
to the very rim of the universe, if one exists

I find myself in non-specific places
where such well-defined locales are irrelevant
mostly inside my own head, but sometimes
floating toward other distant climes
of explosive heat near the big bang

perhaps we are all closer to our own centre
of gravity, down wells of planetary mass
on the same street, feet pressed firmly
to earth, and not aloft, where we might imagine
ourselves to be part of a greater whole

And Again   *Auclair*

tiny planet pulses, waxing in its mother's sun
satellite with ambition, circling
at the tip of its radius vector

as if
tethered by an umbilical cord
capsulate passenger
on course, in transit, tube-fed,
night blood, bone marrow
devours, swells

when sated
it breaks
loose
as if
free
falling
into a broader orbit.

It trumpets autonomy
hitched to the line
that Clotho
spins
spins
spins.

sister planets
trace trajectories that tell of time
on a different scale

on clear nights
earthshine
glows on the waxing moon

how little we'll see of ourselves.

Scars *Auclair*

scars silence blood
shut up leaks and spills
stitch seams on skin
where none should be

scars silence blood
open up floods
of stories
word rivers, pouring out
from throat, bird voice
melody, telling and retelling
events that skin carries
in hues that pale away
until barely seen
which does not mean
invisible, does not mean
there is nothing to see
does not mean
repair occurred

Soot   *Auclair*

What is there to see in the dark
but Chinese shadow puppets playing on a screen?
Light bright as rust corrodes a temporary edge to sadness
a rim of vermillion diluted by tears
eyelashes a somber fringe.

Darkness, never far, sticky as tar
soft as soot, needled
by moonlight, sunlight, flares and flashlights
flaunting no beauty and no shame
heals itself to black.

Kaleidoscope   *Stevenson & Auclair*

A flick of the wrist
and the world
in shards of coloured glass, shifts.

We glean meaning from startling juxtapositions
where we find good company for our journey
and plot our path ahead.

Phrases uttered by other mouths
inform our meanderings
we rotate around a sun, any sun

breaking circles into spirals.
Even if our final destination is certain
nothing is fixed, not even our trajectory

and we may flick our wrists again
for another hope
until, at last, brightness fades.

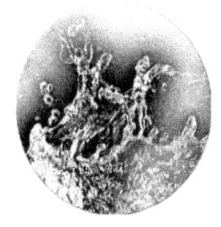

Publication Credits

"A Conversation Between Image-Makers" in *The Maynard* (Canada) 2015

"A Garrisoned Vale" in *Bywords.ca* (Canada) 2021

"A Matter of Intensity" in *MacroMicroCosm* (Canada) 2022

"And Again" in *Fredericksburg Literary and Art Review* (USA) 2016

"Cartographer" in *Young Ravens Review* (USA) 2023

"Comfort Zone" in *MacroMicroCosm* (Canada) 2021

"Composition" in *untethered magazine* (Canada) 2016

"Discovery" in *The BeZine* (USA) 2022

"Down the Pub" in *Blood & Bourbon* (Canada) 2023

"Games We Play" in *Marriage—Lifespan Vol. 6* (Australia) 2022

"Flux" in *Twisted Vine Literary Arts Journal* (USA) 2016

"Heart of Oak" in *Blood & Bourbon* (Canada) 2023

"How to Phrase a Smile" in *Bywords.ca* (Canada) 2017

"Kaleidoscope" in *flo.* (Canada) 2022

"Once Verdant" in *Broadkill Review* (USA) 2019

"Orbits" in *Broadkill Review* (USA) 2019

"Scars" in *Understorey Magazine* (Canada) 2018

"Sign Language" in *Grey Sparrow Journal* (USA) 2023

"Skipping Stones" in *Young Ravens Literary Review* (USA) 2022

"Soot" in *Structo* (UK) 2016

"Stereotype" in *The Elpis Pages* (USA) 2021

"Threadbare" in *The Literary Nest* (USA) 2020

"Trust Fund" in *The BeZine* (USA) 2022

"Unearthing Myself" in *Jaden* (UK) 2021

"Where I Am" in *Jaden* (UK) 2021

About the Authors

Marie-Andrée Auclair's poems have appeared in many print and online publications in recent years. *Bywords.ca* (Canada) was the first magazine to publish her poems. *In/Words Magazine and Press* (Canada) published her first chapbook, *Contrails*, as well as several of her poems. Other poems found homes in Canada, many states of the USA, Europe, UK, Australia and Singapore.

She enjoys hiking, photography, traveling and adding to her culinary repertoire after each trip. She lives in Ottawa, Canada.

Adrienne Stevenson's poems have appeared in many print and online publications in Canada, USA, UK, Europe, India and Australia. Her work appeared first online in 2003, but her entrée into local poetry publications came when she won both first and third place in the *Poets' Pathway: Lampman Challenge* in 2018.

Adrienne lives in Ottawa, Canada. She also writes fiction and creative non-fiction, with several stories and articles published in *Byline* and *Anglo-Celtic Roots*. Her historical novel, *Mirrors & Smoke*, was published in 2023.

When not writing, Adrienne tends a large garden and procrastinates playing several musical instruments.

www.adriennestevenson.ca
www.facebook.com/adriennestevensonwriter

Acknowledgments

First, thanks to the Ottawa Public Library for providing numerous free poetry workshops. There we met a group of poets who have given us steady support for ten years. Our work has benefited thereby. Without their encouragement we would have written and published much less. In particular, we want to recognize the valued and much missed feedback of our friend Randy Droll, who wrote with us for seven of our ten years and sadly passed away in April 2019.

We belong to and participate in other writing groups, including the Canadian Authors Association, Other Tongues, and the online Creative Academy for Writers. Collaboration with colleagues makes us better writers.

Thanks always to family and friends who put up with what they see as an odd hobby.

Also by Adrienne Stevenson

Mirrors & Smoke
Adrienne Stevenson

A story of courage, strength & resilience

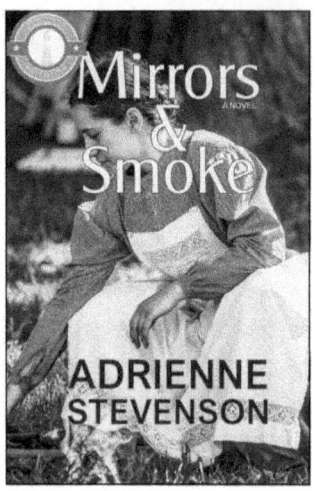

Rebecca Plummer is a herbalist and midwife in Niagara, Upper Canada. Her situation both before and during the War of 1812 is complicated by her feminist attitude and activities to help other women, both of which run counter to the colonial establishment.

Mirrors & Smoke placed third in the Historical Fiction category of the **Pacific Northwest Writers Association** contest.

" Based on real people and historical events, this fictionalized account is told from the Canadian perspective and presents a rarely seen view of life in war-torn, rural Canada. "

- **Donna D. Conrad**, award-winning author *of House of the Moon: Surviving the Sixties* & *The Last Magdalene*

adriennestevenson.ca

Also published by The BumblePuppy Press

(www.bppress.ca/shop)

Carl Dow

- *The Old Man's Last Sauna*
- *Black Grass*
- *Wildflowers: The Women Who Made McCord Chronicle* (forthcoming)
- *Beyond the Blood* (forthcoming)

A. A. Milne

- *The Woke Winnie the Pooh*

Edited, with commentary by Geoffrey Dow (forthcoming)

Zilla Novikov

- *Reprise*

Jules Paivio

- *Life Is Good: A Memoir* (forthcoming)

Rachel A. Rosen

- *Cascade: The Sleep of Reason, Book I*
- *So Human As I Am*
- *Blight: The Sleep of Reason, Book II* (forthcoming)

Dare to discover the *Nightbeats* Extended Universe!

Cascade
Rachel A. Rosen

"Rachel A. Rosen is some kind of twisted genius. I wish I had even half her moves." — Peter Watts

A generation has passed since the Cascade transformed the world, smashing the old political order and infesting the wilderness with demons and shriekgrass. As with the climate crisis that spawned it, emergent magic proved lucky for some, a disaster for many others, and a source of hope and dread for everyone else.

www.bppress.ca

Dare to discover the *Nightbeats* Extended Universe!

Reprise
Zilla Novikov

"... for anyone who appreciates quirkiness of character, sarcasm, irony ... flat out hilarious" — *Amazing Stories*

Time travel, Dungeons & Dragons, infidelity, murder, suicide ... When Dr. François Gagnon offers Eddy Courant a postdoc position studying time loops, the chance to revive her failing career pulls her from depression and makes her feel alive again. But is the cure worse than the disease?

www.bppress.ca

Adventure and romance on the high prairies in 1866

Black Grass
Carl Dow

"If you put James Michener and Louis L'Amour together you get Carl Dow and *Black Grass*." — Maya Zorya Johnson

In 1866, 200 kilometres south of Winnipeg, Susannah Ross was running for her life and running out of time. Close behind were two brutal bounty hunters. Alone and unarmed, Susannah faced 50 years as a bond slave – or worse. Who she find Gabriel Dumont in time to save her, and to warn him of the invasion that was following close behind?

www.bppress.ca

Stories that will move, amuse, and even shock

The Old Man's Last Sauna

Carl Dow

"... this book will make you laugh, think, have fun and ... potentially spook you at times." — *Apt613.com*

From odes to loves found and loves lost, to a clear-eyed look at what it takes to destroy a strong man; from the web of love between a mother and son, to the truths behind a small child's "lies" Carl Dow's debut collection of short fiction offers profound explorations of the human spirit.

www.bppress.ca

Coming soon from The BumblePuppy Press

The Woke Winnie-the-Pooh

A.A. Milne, edited by Geoffrey Dow

The children's classic, re-imagined for the 21st century

As a father of a young daughter, reading *Winnie-the-Pooh* out loud was a disconcerting experience. Why — *why?!?* — is every one of Christopher Robin's toys (except the mother) a boy? If we must label a child's stuffed animals with gender, must they always default to male?

www.bppress.ca

Coming soon from The BumblePuppy Press

Life Is Good: A Memoir
Jules Paivio

The last surviving member of the stories Mackenzie-Papineau Battalian looks back on his life as a social justice warrior

Son of Finnish-Canadian poet and journalist Aku Päiviö, Jules Paivio went to Spain to fight General Francisco Franco's Fascists in 1936. He survived that war, and never looked back from the ideals that drove him there.
This is his story.

www.bppress.ca

The BumblePuppy Press

www.bppress.ca

The BumblePuppy Press

www.bppress.ca

The BumblePuppy Press

www.bppress.ca

www.ingramcontent.com/pod-product-compliance
Lightning Source LLC
Chambersburg PA
CBHW020959090426
42736CB00010B/1388